Reflections

"AN INTRODUCTION TO THE SOUL OF C. D. BROWNER"

By

C. D. Browner, Jr.

ISBN: 0-75962-213-2

This book is printed on acid free paper.

1stBooks - rev. 03/28/01

CONTENTS

A POET'S PRAYER

THANKS GOD
FOR BLESSING ME
WITH A KIND HEART
AND A HUMBLE SPIRIT.

THANK YOU
FOR GIVING ME
A CREATIVE MIND.
MAY YOU ALWAYS BLESS
MY EXPRESSION OF
THE WRITTEN
AND SPOKEN WORD.

BE EVER PRESENT
IN MY HEART.
BE MY STRENGTH
AND MY REMINDER
THAT I AM NEVER
ALONE IN YOU.

C. D. Browner, Jr.

THANK YOU
FOR YOUR BLESSINGS:
PAST, PRESENT,
AND FUTURE.
AMEN.

CLIFFORD BROWNER
7/18/99

POETRY

C. D. Browner, Jr.

AMERICAN FATHERS/
ENDANGERED SPECIES

AMERICAN FATHERS,

UNAMERICAN DREAM,

DISCARDED LOVERS,

SHATTERED DREAMS.

DRIVEN OFF,

WALKED OFF,

AMERICAN FATHERS:

ENDANGERED SPECIES.

PURSUED BY LAW,

LOVER AND WIFE

NOBODY CARES

WHAT HE FEELS INSIDE.

DEADBEAT DAD,

BRANDED FOR LIFE:

AMERICAN FATHER,

ENDANGERED SPECIES.

WANNA KNOW

WHERE YOU BELONG?

WIVES AND CHILDREN

LEFT ALONE.

COME SOMETIME,

OR TELEPHONE;

A FATHER'S PLACE
IS IN THE HOME.

AMERICAN FATHERS,
GET OUT OF BED;
LOVE WITH YOUR HEART;
NOT WITH YOUR HEAD.
PROTECT YOUR BABIES;
THEY'RE YOUR SEED.
AMERICAN FATHERS:
ENDANGERED SPECIES.

AMERICAN FATHERS,
DISPLAY YOUR PRIDE.
IT CAN'T SHINE
LOCKED INSIDE
AMERICAN FATHERS,
REPRESENT;
GET A JOB_
SOME BENEFITS.

SUPPORT YOUR BABIES;
THEY'RE YOUR SEEDS;
UNEDUCATED,
UNLIMITED NEEDS.
SHYLY

JOHN AND RON

AUDITION FOR LIFE;

FAMILIAR SCRIPT,

INSTITUTIONALIZED.

BROKEN_

ANN AND JAN.

BILLY'S PRIZE;

FATHERLESS,

GRANDFATHERLESS,

DREAMLESS EYES.

ABANDONED GENERATION,

STILL THEY BREED;

AMERICAN FATHERS:

AN ENDANGERED SPECIES.

C. D. BROWNER

10/29/99

ANN

ANN WAS A WOMAN
WITH GRACE
AND CHARM;
HER LOVE WAS STRONG
AND WARM.
NO ONE CALLED HER "MOM";
YET HER SPIRIT
WAS LOVING AND CALM.

IT SEEMS THE
GOOD DIE YOUNG,
WHILE THE WEAK
GROW STRONG.

I REMEMBER ANN,
QUIET AND SINCERE, AS
LOVELY AS THE SPRING.
A MAJESTIC QUEEN,
A WOMAN
FILLED WITH DREAMS,
ALWAYS LOVING,
NEVER MEAN,
FAULTLESS AND SERENE.

WHERE SHE PLAYED,

WHEN SHE PLAYED,

SHE GRACED HER WORLD

WITH STYLE.

AND WHEN IT CAME

"HER TIME TO REST,"

ANN LEFT

HER FRIENDS BEGUIDED.

C. D. BROWNER, JR.

10/23/99

C. D. Browner, Jr.

BLUES FOR SUNDAY

THE ROAD OF LIFE
IS A SCARY RIDE.
'ROUND AND ROUND
AND ROUND IT GOES;
WHERE IT STOPS
DON'T NOBODY KNOW.
WE GOT BLUES FOR SUNDAY.

ONE SAID,
"TOUCH THAT TREE
AND YOU WILL DIE."
ONE SAID,
"EAT THAT FRUIT:
IT'LL MAKE YOU WISE."
HE FOOLED ADAM.
HE FOOLED EVE.
WE GOT BLUES FOR SUNDAY.

HEED THE BOOK OF LIFE,
DON'T ROLL THEM DICE.
THE THREE IN THE SKY
HAVE A WATCHFUL EYE.
THEY LOVE YOU,
THEY LOVE ME,
CAN'T YOU SEE?
WE GOT BLUES FOR SUNDAY.

ONE SAID,

"TOUCH THAT TREE

AND YOU WILL DIE."

ONE SAID,

"EAT THAT FRUIT:

IT'LL MAKE YOU WISE."

HE FOOLED ADAM.

HE FOOLED EVE.

HE FOOLED YOU.

HE FOOLED ME.

WE GOT BLUES FOR SUNDAY

C. D. BROWNER, JR.

7/20/99

BORROWED LOVE

LYING HERE' ON THIS BED OF SORROW,
FLIPPING THROUGH THE PAGES OF MY MIND,
I'VE GOT TO GET THINGS STARTED
OR LOSE THIS LONELY HEART OF MINE.
I WORRY ABOUT MY LIFE UPON TOMORROW
AND IF I'M EVER GOING TO FIND
A LOVE I WILL NOT HAVE TO STEAL OR BORROW CAUSE
BORROWED LOVE IS A WASTE OF TIME.

IT'S FIVE A.M. AT MY PITY PARTY.
I NEED YOUR LOVING TOUCH TO SURVIVE.
THE HOST SAYS HE'S REALLY, REALLY, SORRY;
THE HONORED GUEST SHOULD SURELY SOON ARRIVE.
THESE EMPTY ARMS WERE HERE ON CHRISTMAS MORNING;
MY BROKEN HEART WAS SINGING NEW YEARS' BLUES.
SWEETHEART'S DAY JUST ISSUED ME A WARNING:
A BORROWED LOVE WILL GIVE YOUR HEART THE BLUES.

A BORROWED LOVE IS NEVER YOUR POSSESSION;
IT WILL NEVER EVER STAND THE TEST OF TIME.
THE GOD OF LOVE WILL NEVER SMILE UPON YOU;
YOU SHOULD NEVER EVER CROSS THAT SACRED LINE.
A BORROWED LOVE WILL SPOIL YOUR EVERY BLESSING.
A BROKEN HEART YOU ARE ALMOST SURE TO FIND;
IF YOU THINK YOU'LL BECOME THE EXCEPTION,
A FOOL IN LOVE YOU ARE CERTAINLY GOING TO FIND.

CHORUS:

IF BORROWED LOVE IS YOUR HOPE FOR TOMORROW,

THEN HAPPINESS YOU ARE NEVER GOING TO FIND.

A BORROWED LOVE WILL NEVER SOOTHE YOUR SORROWS.

YOUR HEART WILL ALWAYS LIVE ON BORROWED TIME.

C. D. BROWNER JR.

2/9/99

D MAJOR

FROM THE COLLECTION "SONGS FROM THE HEART"

C. D. Browner, Jr.

DON'T FLY OVER NANTUCKET

IT'S NOVEMBER

NINETY-NINE

NEAR'N CURTAINS.

TOO LITTLE TIME,

TOO MUCH UNCERTAIN.

KIDS SHOULDN'T WRITE

ABOUT MURDER AND MAYHEM.

ADULTS SHOULDN'T BEHAVE

LIKE CRABS IN A BUCKET.

PILOTS DON'T FLY YOUR

PLANES OVER NANTUCKET.

C. D. BROWNER, JR.

11/4/99

HEAD-ON COLLISION

FRIDAY NIGHT,

RAINY AND QUIET;

LIKE A CLAP OF THUNDER

TWO CARS COLLIDE;

IN THE DARK OF NIGHT

TWO STRANGERS DIED.

I MUST'VE HAD AN ANGEL

BY MY SIDE.

GOD ONLY KNOWS

HOW I SURVIVED

THAT HEAD-ON COLLISION.

MY MOOD

WAS SOMBER THAT NIGHT.

I FOUGHT WITH MYSELF;

SOMETHING DIDN'T FEEL .RIGHT.

WAS IT DESTINY OR

SOME STRANGE FATE?

I CAN'T RECALL

IF I TOUCHED MY BRAKE.

MY BODY BROKEN INSIDE,

THE PAIN TOLD ME

THAT I SURVIVED

THAT HEAD-ON COLLISION.

IN REALITY_

IT'S LIKE A DREAM.

MY MEMORY

OF NURSES, DOCTORS,

X-RAY MACHINES,

FRIENDS, FAMILY, AND

SURGEON TEAMS.

I AM BETTER NOW;

THE PAIN IS GONE.

THANKS FOR THE CARDS;

TO THE ONES WHO PHONED,

MY LOVE GOES OUT, TO

THE KNOWN AND UNKNOWN.

CONSEQUENTLY,

LIVES WERE CHANGED

THAT NIGHT,

CERTAINLY FOR THE LIVING.

I TOOK A CLOSER LOOK INSIDE;

I GOT A SECOND CHANCE.

I GOT A SECOND CHANCE!

WHEN I SURVIVED,

THAT HEAD-ON COLLISION,

I SURVIVED,

THAT HEAD-ON COLLISION.

C. D. BROWNER, JR.

10/11/99

GOD'S LOVE

GOD IS ALWAYS IN HIS PLACE;

EVEN ON THOSE RAINY DAYS.

THE CLOUDS THAT SWIRL SO HIGH ABOVE

ARE SMALL REMINDERS OF GOD'S LOVE?

CLIFFORD BROWNER

1022/98

TWO EYES AWAY

ON THE DARKEST SUNNY DAY,
I CAN SEE TWO EYES AWAY.
THEY WATCH ME SLEEP,
THEY WATCH ME PRAY;
THEY EVEN WATCH ME
AS I SAY,
"I CAN SEE TWO EYES AWAY."

CLIFFORD BROWNER
10/29/98

ON LOVE

SOMEHOW LOVE
HAS COME BETWEEN US;
INSTEAD OF LOVE
I FEEL DISTRUST.
I PRAY SOMEDAY
OUR SUNS WILL SHINE;
I'LL LIGHT YOUR DAY,
AND YOU'LL LIGHT MINE.

CLIFFORD BROWNER
10/22/98

HOMEMAKER

HOMEMAKER,
LOVE OF MY LIFE.
SOMEDAY, SOMEHOW,
YOU'LL SHARE MY LIFE,

CARETAKER,
HEARTBREAKER,
MY LOVEMAKER;
I DREAM OF YOU
NIGHT AND DAY.

WITH A LOVE, AS
DEEP AS THE SEA.
MY HOMEMAKER,
MY LOVE, AND ME.

C. D. BROWNER, JR.
10/27/99

IF HEAVEN MOVES

IF HEAVEN MOVES
LEST I STARE;
WHERE WILL IT MOVE?
SOMEWHERE OUT THERE?
SO BIG AND WIDE
ARE HEAVEN'S SKIES;
A MOVE WOULD FOOL
TEN THOUSAND EYES.

CLIFFORD BROWNER
10/22/98

SHEE NEEDS A LIFE

SHE MAY NOT SEE YOU EVERY DAY,
BUT WHEN SHE DOES SHE WANTS TO PLAY.
SHE FEELS SHE'S RUNNING OUT OF TIME;
FRIENDS OF HERS ARE BUSY DYING.

NOTHING'S PLAYING ON TV,
SEX AND VIOLENCE IS ALL SHE CAN SEE.
SHE'LL NEVER MAKE IT TO THE TOP.
SHE'LL KEEP ON WORK'N TIL SHE DROPS.

SISTER'S PLAYING HARD TO GET.
SHE'D RATHER LOVE A HAIRY PET.
SHE WANTS TO TRAVEL TO AND FRO,
NO MAN AT HOME TO ASK TO GO.

SHE'S BEEN PREGANT TWICE BEFORE,
WHO THE FATHER IS, SHE DOESN'T KNOW.
CHILDREN SLEEPING ON THE FLOOR,
SHE NEEDS A MAN TO CHANGE HER FLOW.

NO ONE AT HOME TO SHARE THE RENT.
HER WELFARE CHECK IS HEAVEN SENT.
BEFORE IT COMES THE MONEY'S SPENT.
HER LONG BLOND WEAVE IS FULL OF LINT.

SHE SAYS SHE WEARS A TWENTY-FOUR;

SHE PASSED THAT SIZE A YEAR AGO.

SHE HAS NO ONE TO CALL HER OWN.

HER ONLY FRIEND'S HER TELEPHONE.

SHE DRINKS AND SMOKES WHILE TRYING TO COPE.

HER TWELVE YEAR OLD IS PUSHING DOPE,

NO FATHER IMAGE TO BE FOUND;

SHE KNOWS ONE DAY HE'S GOING DOWN.

BEEN DOWN SO LONG STILL WASTING TIME,

BABY'S SICK HASN'T GOT A DIME,

SOMETIMES SHE CRYS HERSELF TO SLEEP

TO DROWN THE NOISE DOWN ON THE STREET.

SHE NEEDS A LIFE. SHE NEEDS A LIFE.

C. D. BROWNER, JR.

8/10/98

FROM THE COLLECTION "SAD MANS BLUES"

SON OF MINE

STANDING THERE ON THE EDGE OF TIME,
HE THINKS HE'S HIS; I KNOW HE'S MINE.
STILL SO YOUNG, AND YET SO FINE,
I SWEAR B Y GOD, HE'S A SON OF MINE.

BRUISED BY PAIN HE PLOTS HIS GAME.
HE MUST BE TOUGH, OR SHOW UP LAME.
FOR THE PATH HE CHOSE, I TAKE THE BLAME.
SMOKES AND STUFF HAVE MARRED HIS BRAIN.

HE DRAINS MY PRIDE WITH WHAT HE STYLES:
RINGS AND CHAINS AND GANGSTER RIDES.
IS IT LOVE HE NEEDS, OR INTIMIDATION?
IS HIS HONEST TRUTH, INCRIMINATION?

IT ISN'T ALL HIS FAULT; IT'S THE GENERATION.
HAVING BEEN YOUNG, I KNOW HIS FRUSTRATION.
THROUGH GOOD AND BAD, IN SIN OR CRIME,
I SWEAR BY GOD, HE'S A SON OF MINE.

WHEN YOU STAKE YOUR CLAIM ON TURF ACROSS TOWN,
REMEMBER FOR LOVE, DAD'S ALWAYS DOWN.
WEATHER WORTH A MILLION, OR ONE THIN DIME,
I SWEAR BY GOD, HE'S A SON OF MINE.

I LOVE YOU SON,

YOUR DAD

CLIFFORD BROWNER

1/6/99

FROM THE COLLECTION "SAD MANS BLUES"

C. D. Browner, Jr.

THE CHINABERRY TREE

HIGH NEAR THE TOP, WHERE
THE MOCKINGBIRD SINGS,
THERE, I'D CLIMB
TO TRY MY WINGS.
MY TRUMPET TRILLED,
THE HIGH NOTES RANG,
PLAY'N LIFE'S LITTLE THEME.
I MISS MY LOVE, MY FIRST LOVE,
MY LONE SUMMER DREAM.

SOMETIMES I TALKED TO GOD;
SOMETIMES JUST TO ME,
SOMETIMES TO MY BEST FRIEND,
THE CHINABERRY TREE.
FIFTEEN FEET TALL,
LIMBS SPREAD WIDE,
I TOLD IT MY SECRETS
I SHARED THEM WITH PRIDE.

ITS BERRIES WERE GREEN;
THEN YELLOW, THEN BROWN.
THE BERRIES THAT HAD HUNG HIGH;
FELL LIFELESS TO THE GROUND.
WHEN THE EVENING CAME
I'D CLIMB TO THE GROUND.

I LONGED FOR MY FRIEND,

AS THE SUN WENT DOWN.

C. D. BROWNER, JR.

12/5/99

THE MORNING SUN

LORD, FORGIVE YOUR CHILD, THE SINNER;
LORD, I'VE GOT THIS RACE TO RUN.
LORD, I'LL KNOW THAT I'M FORGIVEN
WHEN I SEE THE MORNING SUN.

SOMETIMES MY ROAD IS ROCKY;
SOMETIMES MY LIFE COMES UNDONE.
I KNOW YOU'LL BE AT THE RIVER
WHEN I SEE THE MORNING SUN.

THE MORNING SUN IS SO SPECIAL;
IT LETS ME KNOW THE NIGHT IS DONE.
LORD, I'LL KNOW YOU DIDN'T FORGET ME
WHEN I SEE THE MORNING SUN.

GOD FORGIVES MY EVERY TRESPASS,
FOR REASONS I DON'T UNDERSTAND. BUT,
I KNOW HE'S STILL IN HEAVEN
WHEN I SEE THE MORNING SUN.

CLIFFORD BROWNER
7/24/99

THE PASSER-BY

DAWN IS DAWN'N
AS I RISE.
A FAMILIAR STRANGER,
PASSER-BY,
I GLIMPSED HIM
THROUGH MY MIND'S EYE.
I LIKED HIS LOOK;
I LOVED HIS STYLE.
I WISH'D HE'D STOP
AND CHAT AWHILE.
ECHOES FROM HIS
FOOTSTEPS TOLD
THE ESSENCE OF
HIS LIVELY STROLL
A GLANCE INTO
THE STRANGER'S EYE
REVEALED TO ME
THE PASSER-BY.

CLIFFORD D. BROWNER
11/3/99

THE QUESTION

WHERE IN YOUR KINGDOM

DOES MY SOUL RESIDE?

IN HEAVEN, OR EARTH?

SOME DISTANCE SKIES?

WHO AM I?

IF I MAY INQUIRE?

THE WHO,

THE WHAT,

THE WHEN,

THE WHY...

WHY WAS I BORN?

WHY MUST I DIE?

I POSE THESE QUESTIONS

WHERE I STAND.

AM I A SPIRIT

OR JUST A MAN?

WHERE DO I FIT

IN YOUR MASTER PLAN?

CLIFFORD BROWNER

12/27/98

ON PRAISE

YOU ARE NOT
THE MASTER'S TOY.
TO SEE YOU BREAK
BRINGS HIM NO JOY.
IF YOU FALL,
HE'LL PICK YOU UP;
YOU'LL NEVER DRINK
THE BITTER CUP.
IN YOUR PRAISE,
LIFT HIM UP.
GIVE HIM YOUR PRAISE
THAT'S ENOUGH.

CLIPFORD BROWNER
10/98

TO THE PROUD

I SAY TO YOU,

"PROUD MADAM,"

"PROUD SIR,"

WHO CHOOSE TO

BRAG OR BOAST;

DON'T BE

DISALLUSIONED

BY THE CARDS

YOU HOLD.

THE ONLY

DIFFERENCE

BETWEEN THEIRS

AND YOURS

IS YOURS IS MOSTLY

YOURS.

C. D. BROWNER, JR.

11/9/99

UNTITLED

AT THIS POINT IN MY LIFE
I'M AT THE ROADS OF THE BISECTION (INTERSECTION)

LORD GIVE ME SOME DIRECTION
A SIMPLE VOICE INFLECTION
OR BETTER YET SOME PROTECTION

AM I MISSING MY BLESSINGS
CAUGHT UP IN THE SESSION
TOO AFRAID OF CONFESSION
SINFUL THOUGHTS MANIFESTIN'

A LIFE OR DEATH QUESTION
DO I REALLY WANNA HEAR YES
OR SEE AN END TO MY QUEST
THE FEELIN' IN MY CHEST
THAT WON'T LET ME REST
GOT ME ____ING FAMILY LIKE INCEST

BUT IN THE SENSE OF THE WORD
BUT NOT THE TENSE OF THE VERB

I SMELL
THE SCENTS OF THE HERB
GOT MY MENTAL ON SWERVE

BUT WILL I REACH THAT CURB
AND SEE THE PURPOSE THAT IT SERVES

IN COMPLIANCE TO THAT
I'M IN DEFIANCE OF FACT
AND MANY TIE-INS TO CRACK
THE SIZE OF THE SACK
GOT MY EYES ON THE STACK

BUT REALLY CAN I MAKE THE LONG
ROAD BACK...

JONATHAN BROWNER
SUBMITTED BY: CLIFFORD BROWNER
12/98
FROM THE COLLECTION "SAD MANS BLUES"

WATCHMAN OF THE NIGHT

BENEATH
THE RESTLESS MOON,
THE WATCHMAN
OUT OF SIGHT,
MY LOVE AND I
SAT IN THE DARK,
LOOKING
FOR THE LIGHT.

THE NIGHT WAS YOUNG.
IN EARLY SPRING;
THE ROSE HAD DARNED
ITS BUDS.

THE WATCHMAN SMILED.
I KISSED HER LIPS,
AND MUCH TO HIS
DELIGHT, HE WATCHED
THE GLOW OF LOVE,
LIGHT
THE PITCH BLACK
NIGHT.

WE HELD EACH OTHER
WHAT SEEMED TO ME,
A UNIVERSAL HOUR;
OUR LOVE BLOOMED
AND BECAME,
AN ETERNAL FLOWER.

THE WATCHMAN YAWNED;
HIS LIGHT WENT OUT:
FOR LOVE HAD CLAIMED
HIS POWER.

C. D. BROWNER, JR.
SUMMER, 1999

WATER WATER

MY MOUTH IS DRY,
FROM THE DUST
OF THE ROAD.
WATER! WATER!
BATHE MY SOUL.

WATER, WATER,
FROM
THE FOUNTAIN
FLOW;
FILL MY SOUL,
I THIRST NO MORE.

C. D. BROWNER, JR.
FALL 1999

C. D. Browner, Jr.

GOSPEL SONG LYRICS

C. D. Browner, Jr.

A GREATER STATE OF GRACE

GRACE, GRACE, OH GOD'S GRACE,

A GREATER STATE OF GRACE.

GRACE, GRACE OH GOD'S GRACE,

A GREATER STATE OF GRACE.

NO MORE TEARS AND NO MORE PAIN,

WHEN WE HEAR THE ANGELS SING;

IN GOD'S KINGDOM IN THE SKY,

NO MORE TOILS AND NO MORE STRIFE,

THE GIFT OF GOD IS ETERNAL LIFE;

ENDLESS JOY AND ENDLESS PRAISE,

TRUST IN GOD YOUR SOUL HE'LL SAVE.

ONLY GOD CAN GIVE YOU GRACE,

PUT YOUR HAND IN JESUS' HAND.

JEWS AND GENTILES, FRIENDS AND FOE,

LET GOD'S SPIRIT TAKE CONTROL;

GOD IS COMING ON JUDGEMENT DAY

TO REIGN FOREVER MORE.

HALLELUJAH, GRACE, GRACE, OH GOD'S GRACE,

IN THE MORNING, GRACE, GRACE, OH GOD'S GRACE,

BORN AGAIN AN IMMORTAL SOUL,
SANCTIFIED WITH THE HOLY GHOST,
WALKING WITH GOD ON STREETS OF GOLD,

CHORUS: A GREATER STATE OF GRACE
HALLELUJAH, GRACE, GRACE, OH GOD'S GRACE
A GREATER STATE OF GRACE,
IN THE MORNING, GRACE, GRACE, OH GOD'S GRACE
A GREATER STATE OF GRACE.

"C. D. BROWNER, JR.
1/26/2000 EM"

CROSSROAD

LORD MY LIFE IS SO FULL OF SORROW;
I LONG FOR HEAVEN AND HOME.
I HAVE TRAVELED THE WHOLE WORLD OVER,
TRYING TO GET BACK HOME.
I HAVE COME OVER HILLS AND MOUNTAINS,
THROUGH RAIN, WINDS AND STORMS.
NOW I HAVE COME TO A CROSSROAD ON MY JOURNEY;
TELL ME, WHICH ROAD WILL LEAD ME HOME.

OH SOMETIMES MY LOAD GOT SO HEAVY,
SOMETIMES I WOULD STUMBLE AND FALL,
SOMETIMES MY WAY WAS DARK AND DREARY,
I WONDERED IF I'D EVER GET HOME.
LORD I DON'T KNOW MY TRUE CONDITION;
TELL ME, AM I WEAK OR STRONG.
I HAVE COME TO A CROSSROAD ON MY JOURNEY;
TELL ME, WHICH ROAD WILL LEAD ME HOME.

NOW AND THEN I TELL MYSELF NOT TO WORRY,
WHEN I'VE DONE THE VERY BEST THAT I CAN.
I KNOW THE LORD WILL BEAR MY HEAVY BURDEN,
IF I TRUST IT IN HIS HAND.
IN PAIN AND TEARS I TRAVELED ON THIS JOURNEY,
HEADED FOR THE PROMISED LAND,
NOW I HAVE COME TO A CROSSROAD ON MY JOURNEY,
TELL ME, WHICH ROAD WILL LEAD ME HOME.

I'VE BEEN TRIED, TRAVELING ON THIS JOURNEY.

I GOT LOST ON A STORMY SEA.

THAT OLD DEVIL HAD A HOLD ON ME;

AND HE WOULD NOT SET ME FREE.

I PRAYED TO GOD FOR NEW DIRECTION.

I BELIEVE HE HEARD MY PLEA.

NOW I HAVE COME TO A CROSSROAD ON MY JOURNEY,

I KNOW THE LORD WILL GUIDE MY FEET.

CLIFFORD BROWNER

8/16/98

D MAJOR

FROM THE COLLECTION "SONGS FROM THE HEART"

DOWN IN MY SOUL

THE LOVE HE GIVES
IT IS SO REAL
I CAN FEEL IT
DOWN IN MY SOUL.

THE PEACE HE GIVES
IT IS SO REAL
I CAN FEEL IT DOWN
IN MY SOUL.

THE JOY HE GIVES
IT IS SO REAL
I CAN FEEL IT
DOWN IN MY SOUL.

CHORUS:
DOWN IN MY SOUL
DOWN IN MY SOUL
MY GOD HE LIVES
DOWN IN MY SOUL.

HE HEALED MY BODY
AND HE MADE ME WHOLE
NOW MY GOD LIVES
DOWN IN MY SOUL.

C. D. Browner, Jr.

MY GOD IS PEACE
HE IS JOY AND LOVE.
HE IS THE FIRE,
THE WATER AND THE BLOOD.
HE'S THE FATHER, SON
AND THE HOLY GHOST.
HE IS THE FOUNTAIN
WHERE LIVING WATERS FLOW.
HE IS THE SPIRIT,
DOWN IN MY SOUL

CLIFFORD BROWNER
7/28/2000
A MAJOR

GOING HOME TO LIVE WITH MY LORD

I LIVED A LIFE OF SIN,

BUT LORD I'VE MADE A CHANGE.

I LIVED A LIFE OF SIN,

BUT LORD I'VE MADE A CHANGE.

I MADE A CHANGE IN MY JESUS NAME.

I MADE A CHANGE IN MY JESUS NAME.

THEY'RE SINGING AND SHOUTING OVER THERE,

WHERE JESUS LIVE.

THEY'RE SINGING AND SHOUTING OVER THERE,

WHERE JESUS LIVE.

I'M GOING HOME TO LIVE WITH MY LORD,

I'M GOING HOME TO LIVE WITH MY LORD.

THEY'RE SERVING MILK AND HONEY OVER THERE,

WHERE JESUS LIVE.

THEY'RE SERVING MILK AND HONEY OVER THERE,

WHERE JESUS LIVE.

I'M GOING HOME TO LIVE WITH MY LORD.

I'M GOING HOME TO LIVE WITH MY LORD.

I'VE GOT A MOTHER AND FATHER OVER THERE,

WHERE JESUS LIVE.

I'VE GOT A MOTHER AND FATHER OVER THERE,

WHERE JESUS LIVE.

I'M GOING HOME TO LIVE WITH MY LORD.

I'M GOING HOME TO LIVE WITH MY LORD.

THERE IS NO MORE DYING OVER THERE,
WHERE JESUS LIVE.
THERE IS NO WORK DYING OVER THERE,
WHERE JESUS LIVE.
I'M GOING HOME TO LIVE WITH MY LORD.
I'M GOING HOME TO LIVE WITH MY LORD.

DON'T YOU WANT TO GO,
WHERE JESUS LIVE?
DON'T YOU WANT TO GO,
WHERE JESUS LIVE?
I'M GOING HOME TO LIVE WITH MY LORD,
I'M GOING HOME TO LIVE WITH MY LORD.

CHORUS:
MY JESUS PAID THE PRICE, SO THAT I COULD RIDE
MY JESUS PAID THE PRICE; SO THAT I COULD RIDE,
THAT HEAVEN BOUND SHIP IN THE SKY.
LORD, THIS OLD WORLD'S FULL OF TROUBLE,
BEFORE MY SOUL GET LOST,
LORD, THIS OLD WORLD'S FULL OP TROUBLE.
BEFORE MY SOUL GETS LOST,
I'M GOING HOME TO LIVE WITH MY LORD.
I'M GOING HOME TO LIVE WITH MY LORD.

CLIFFORD BROWNER (E MINOR) 10/21/98

HIS BLOOD RAINS DOWN ON ME

WHEN STORM CLOUDS RISE
AND LOUD THUNDER ROAR;
I DON'T GET DISCOURAGED.
CAUSE HEAVEN KNOWS.
WITH A RAINBOW OF LOVE
GOD PROMISED US LIFE;
AND FOR MY SALVATION
MY LORD BLED AND DIED.
GOD'S LOVE KNOWS NO LIMITS
LIKE STARS IN THE SKIES;
WHEN HIS BLOOD RAINS DOWN
ON ME. ON ME.

AND WHEN I'M ALONE,
SAD TIMES IN MY LIFE,
NO MATTER WHAT THE TROUBLE,
I KNOW THAT GOD'S ON MY SIDE.
IN TIMES OF GLADNESS
MY HAPPY HEART CRIES;
HE'LL TAKE ME TO HEAVEN,
HIS HOME ABOVE THE CLOUDS.
GOD'S LOVE KNOWS NO LIMITS
LIKE STARS IN THE SKIES;
WHEN HIS BLOOD RAINS DOWN,
ON ME. ON ME.

SO DON'T STOP THE RAIN.

LET THE LOUD THUNDER ROAR.

LET THE STORM CLOUDS RISE.

LET THE STRONG WINDS BLOW.

LET THE RAIN COME DOWN;

TIL THE SEAS OVER FLOW,

TIL HIS BLOOD RAINS DOWN

ON ME. ON ME.

TIL HIS BLOOD RAINS DOWN

ON ME. ON ME.

C. D. BROWNER, JR.

HIS HOLY PLACE

I'VE GOT TWO HANDS, TWO HANDS,

TO WORK FOR MY JESUS.

I'VE GOT TWO FEET, TWO FEET,

TO RUN FOR THE LORD.

I'VE GOT TWO EARS, TWO EARS,

TO HEAR HIS WORD FROM HEAVEN.

I WANT TO LIVE FOREVER IN HIS HOLY PLACE.

I'VE GOT ONE LIFE; ONE LIFE,

TO LIVE FOR MY JESUS.

I' V GOT ONE SOUL; ONE SOUL

TO SAVE FROM SIN.

I'VE GOT ONE CHANCE; ONE CHANCE,

TO STEAL AWAY TO HEAVEN.

I WANT TO LIVE FOREVER IN HIS HOLY PLACE.

I'VE GOT ONE TONGUE; ONE TONGUE,

TO CONFESS MY FAITH IN JESUS.

I'VE GOT ONE VOICE, ONE VOICE,

TO SING HIS PRAISE

I'VE GOT TWO EYES, TWO EYES,

TO SEE HIS FACE IN HEAVEN.

I WANT TO LIVE FOREVER IN HIS HOLY PLACE.

I NEED ONE CROWN
WHEN I GET TO HEAVEN.
I NEED ONE ROBE
TO CLOTHE MY SOUL
I NEED NEW SHOES
TO WALK AROUND IN HEAVEN.
I WANT TO LIVE FOREVER IN HIS HOLY PLACE.

GOD SAID, A LIAR WON'T MAKE IT. WON'T MAKE IT. WON'T MAKE IT
A THIEF, WON'T MAKE IT. WON'T MAKE IT. WON'T MAKE IT.
A BACKSLIDER, WON'T MAKE IT. WON'T MAKE IT. WON'T MAKE IT.
THE JEALOUS HEARTED, WON'T MAKE IT. WON'T MAKE IT. WON'T MAKE IT.
A DRUNKARD, WON'T MAKE IT. WON'T MAKE IT. WON'T MAKE IT.
A MURDERER, SURE WON'T MAKE IT. WON'T MAKE IT. WON'T MAKE IT.
THE SUNDAY CHRISTIAN, OH WON'T MAKE IT. WON'T MAKE IT. WON'T MAKE IT.
I'VE GOT TO LIVE FOREVER IN HIS HOLY PLACE.

CLIFFORD BROWNER
A MAJOR
2/10/99
FROM THE COLLECTION "FIRST BLOOD"

I'M JUST A MAN

LORD, WHENEVER I GET LONELY,

WILL YOU BE MY FRIEND?

LORD, WHEN I GROW TIRED AND WEARY,

WILL YOU LEND A HAND?

AND LORD, WHEN I'VE DONE ALL I CAN,

WILL YOU UNDERSTAND?

LORD, YOU MADE ME FROM THE DUST.

YOU MADE ME WITH YOUR HANDS.

YOU SAID IF I BELIEVE IN YOU,

YOU WOULD LET ME LIVE AGAIN.

SO LORD, PLEASE DISCIPLINE ME DAILY;

TO DO THE THINGS YOU COMMAND?

LORD, WHEN ALL MY DEEDS ARE NUMBERED,

REMEMBER I'M JUST A MAN?

PLEASE MOTIVATE ME FATHER

TO GLORIFY AND PRAISE YOUR NAME?

PLEASE CONSECRATE MY SPIRIT

WITH THE SACRED BLOOD OF THE LAMB?

AND LORD, WHEN THE BOOK OF LIFE IS OPENED

AND THE ANGELS CALL MY NAME,

AND LORD, WHEN ALL MY DEEDS ARE NUMBERED,

REMEMBER I'M JUST A MAN?

LORD YOU PLACED AT MY COMMAND;
THE BIRDS, THE BEASTS, THE TREES AND THE LAND.
LORD YOU GAVE YOUR ONLY SON
FOR RANSOM AND MY BOND.
I BELIEVE YOU LIVED, BLED AND DIED,
SO I COULD LIVE WITH YOU IN PARADISE.

SO LORD, WHEN I TURN TO CHEATING AND LYING,
AND THE LOVE IN ME IS DYING,
AND THE ONLY VOICE I HEAR IS MINE.
WHEN I CHANGE MY WICKED WAYS
AND I SEEK OUT YOUR FACE,
AND MY DESTINY IS IN YOUR HANDS,
LORD REMEMBER, I'M JUST A MAN?
PLEASE REMEMBER I'M JUST A MAN?

C. D. BROWNER, JR. (8/27/99) FROM
"QUIET PRAISE" G MAJOR

LIGHT FROM HEAVEN

LIGHT FROM HEAVEN,
SHINE ON ME.
LIGHT FROM HEAVEN,
SHINE ON ME.
LIGHT FROM HEAVEN,
SHINE ON ME.
LORD, LET YOUR LIGHT,
SHINE ON ME?

LIGHT FROM HEAVEN,
SHINE ON ME.
YOUR BLINDING LIGHT LORD
MADE ME SEE.
LIGHT FROM HEAVEN,
SHINE ON ME.
LORD, LET YOUR LIGHT,
SHINE ON ME?

OH, HOLY SPIRIT,
ABIDE IN ME.
I'LL SPREAD YOUR WORD LORD,
FROM SEA TO SEA.
LIGHT FROM HEAVEN,
SHINE ON ME.
LORD, LET YOUR LIGHT,
SHINE ON ME?

I'M YOUR VESSEL,

SHINE ON ME

GRANT THE JEWS AND GENTILES

EVERLASTING PEACE.

LIGHT FROM HEAVEN,

SHINE ON ME.

LORD, LET YOUR LIGHT,

SHINE ON ME?

CLIFFORD BROWNER

E MAJOR

10/7/98

FROM THE COLLECTION "FIRST BLOOD"

LONELY SOLDIER, LOVING MOTHER

LONELY SOLDIER, LOVING MOTHER,
UP IN HEAVEN SOMEWHERE.
I HAVE FELT YOUR PRESENCE,
SINCE MY CHILDHOOD;
KEEP ME EVER IN YOUR CARE.

LONELY SOLDIER, LOVING MOTHER,
GUIDE ME THUR THE TOILS AND SNARES.
I.LEARNED LOVE AT YOUR BOSOM.
YOU TAUGHT ME TO PRAY,
THAT KEEPS ME SAFE FROM DANGER
FROM DAY TO DAY.

YOUR MEMORY IS PRECIOUS.
YOUR LOVE IS DIVINE;
YOUR LIGHT WILL FOREVER SHINE.
YOU LIVED A LIFE OF VIRTURE,
TEMPERED WITH LOVE.
THE VICTORY WILL BE YOURS IN ZION.

LONELY SOLDIER, LOVING MOTHER
WAITING IN HEAVEN SOMEWHERE.

I CAN FEEL YOUR PRESENCE
EVER NEAR ME,
KEEP ME EVER IN YOUR CARE.

C. D. BROWNER
G MAJOR
MARCH 2000

MAKE IT CLEAR

PLEASE. MAKE IT CLEAR, LORD,
PLEASE, MAKE IT PLAIN?
YOU ARE MY SAVIOR,
I'LL PRAISE YOUR NAME.
I PRAY FOR MERCY,
LOVE, TRUTH AND GRACE,
MAKE ME WHOLE, LORD,
RENEW MY FAITH.

PLEASE MAKE IT CLEAR, LORD,
PLEASE MAKE IT PLAIN?
YOU ARE MY SAVIOR
I'LL PRAISE YOUR NAME.
AND WHEN MY LIFE, LORD,
IS ALMOST GONE,
PLEASE SAVE MY SOUL,
PLEASE TAKE ME HOME?

MY DYING HOUR
IS DRAWING NEAR.
I FEEL YOUR POWER,
I KNOW YOU ARE HERE.
I'VE LIVED MY LIFE
NEVER SINCERE,
NOW AT THE THOUGHT, LORD,
I TREMBLE IN FEAR.

OH HOLY FATHER,

MY LORD, MY GOD,

CONSIDER MY LABOR;

PLEASE SEARCH MY HEART?

CHASTISE ME FATHER

WITH MERCY AND LOVE,

YOU BORE MY BURDEN,

I'M WASHED IN YOUR BLOOD.

PLEASE MAKE IT CLEAR, LORD,

PLEASE MAKE IT PLAIN?

YOU ARE MY SAVIOR,

I'LL PRAISE YOUR NAME.

PLEASE MAKE IT CLEAR, LORD,

PLEASE MAKE IT PLAIN?

YOU ARE MY SAVIOR

I'LL PRAISE, YOUR NAME.

C. D. BROWNER, JR.

4/6/99

C MAJOR

FROM THE COLLECTION

"SONGS FROM THE HEART"

ONE BREATH

WE'RE ONE BREATH FROM HEAVEN;
ONE BREATH AWAY FROM GOD.
WE'RE ONE BREATH FROM HEAVEN;
ONE BREATH AND LIFE IS GONE.

YOU'VE GOT TO LEARN TO LOVE YOUR ENEMIES,
YOU'VE GOT TO RID YOUR LIFE OF SIN.
SALVATION IS THE KEY TO HEAVEN,
GOD SAID HE'S COMING AGAIN.

YOU'VE GOT TO LEARN TO LOVE YOUR NEIGHBOR
EVEN WHEN HE'S NOT YOUR FRIEND,
NEVER END YOUR DAYS IN TROUBLE,
YOU DON'T KNOW WHEN YOUR LIFE WILL END.

NEVER WORSHIP WORLDLY POSSESSIONS;
OR MAKE A GOD OF BEAST OR MEN.
SEEK THE LORD WITH PRAYER AND SUPPLICATION;
FOR ONLY PEACE AND LOVE WILL WIN.

LIFE IS NOT A PRIVATE POSSESSION;
BUT YOU CAN CHOOSE THE WAY IT ENDS.
IT TAKES ONE BREATH TO ASK GODS FORGIVENESS;
OR ONE BREATH TO DIE IN SIN.

WE'RE ONE BREATH FROM HEAVEN;
ONE BREATH AWAY FROM GOD.
WE'RE ONE BREATH FROM HEAVEN,
ONE BREATH AND LIFE IS GONE.

CLIFFORD BROWNER
1/25/99
A MAJOR
FROM THE COLLECTION "FIRST BLOOD"
COPYRIGHTS RESERVED 1999

"PRAYER "

PRAYER IS A PETITION
FOR A CLOSER WALK WITH GOD;
PRAYER IS A PLEA
TO A GRACIOUS AWESOME GOD;
PRAYER, OF THE RIGHTEOUS,
AVAILETH MUCH WITH GOD;

YOU CAN'T SAY YOU SERVE HIM
WHEN YOUR WORK IS UNDONE.
YOU CAN'T TRULY PRAISE HIM
WHEN YOUR FAITH IN HIM IS GONE;
AND YOU CAN'T SAY YOU LOVE HIM
WITH A LYING TONGUE,

GOD PRAYED TO GOD,
TO SAVE A SINFUL LAND.
GOD PRAYED TO GOD,
FOR THE SOULOF EVERY MAN.
GOD PRAYED TO GOD,
SO WE WOULD UNDERSTAND,

HE IS ALPHA AND OMEGA.
HE IS AN EVERLASTING ARM.
HE IS THE LILLYOF THE VALLEY.

HE IS THE BEGOTTEN SON.
ASK AND HE WILL GIVE YOU
THE DESIRES OF YOUR HEART.

PRAYER, PLACES MAN
ON A ONE ON ONE WITH GOD.
PRAYER, PLACES MAN
ABOVE THE MOON, SUN AND STARS.
PRAYER, PLACES MAN
ON THE VERY HEART OF GOD.

CHORUS:
WE'VE GOT TO KEEP ON PRAY'N,
KEEP ON PRAY'N,
TIL HIS WILL BE DONE

C. D. BROWNER
10/12/00 REVISED 10/17/00
G MAJOR

SAVE ME

FLOWERS STILL GROW

WHERE MAN NEVER SOWED;

AND THE LORD GAVE HIS LIFE ON A HILL.

AND THE BEAUTY OF IT ALL,

WE WILL ALL HEAR HIS CALL,

WHEN THE GLORY OF THE LORD COMES DOWN.

AS EACH NEW DAY ENDS,

I'LL ASK FORGIVENESS FOR MY SINS.

LORD, PLEASE HEAR MY PRAYER,

SAVE ME? SAVE ME! SAVE ME!

GOD ONLY KNOWS

WHY THE GREEN GRASS GROW;

AND THE LILLIES GROW WILD IN THE FIELD.

AS THE SUN STANDS HIGH AT NOON,

YOU CAN SEE THEM ALL ABLOOM;

WHEN THE GLORY OF THE LORD COMES DOWN.

AND AS EACH NEW DAY ENDS,

I'LL ASK FORGIVENESS FOR MY SINS.

LORD, PLEASE HEAR MY PRAYER,

SAVE ME? SAVE ME! SAVE ME!

THE WILD BEAST THAT FEED

ON FLOWERS AND TREES,

FIND SHADE AND FULFILL THEIR NEEDS.

GOD SENDS HIS LOVE ON THE WINGS OF A DOVE;
WHEN THE GLORY OF THE LORD COMES DOWN.
AND AS EACH NEW DAY ENDS,
I'LL ASK FORGIVENESS FOR MY SINS.
LORD, PLEASE HEAR MY PRAYER,
SAVE ME? SAVE ME! SAVE ME!
SAVE ME? SAVE ME! SAVE ME!
LORD, PLEASE HEAR MY PRAYER,
SAVE ME?

CLIFFORD BROWNER
D MAJOR
3/96
FROM THE COLLECTION "FIRST BLOOD"

THE ARMOR OF GOD

I'M GOING TO PUT ON THE WHOLE ARMOR OF GOD.
I'M GOING TO PUT ON THE WHOLE ARMOR OF GOD.
I'M GOING TO PUT ON THE WHOLE ARMOR OF GOD;
SO I CAN STAND WHEN EVIL COMES.

MY LOINS ARE GIRT WITH TRUTH AND LOVE.
IT GIVES ME STRENGTH; I FEEL GOD'S LOVE.
MY LOINS ARE GIRT WITH TRUTH AND LOVE;
SO I CAN STAND WHEN EVIL COMES.

A BREASTPLATE OF RIGHTEOUSNESS PROTECTS MY SOUL;
FROM THE FIERY DARTS THAT THE DEVIL THROWS.
A BREASTPLATE OF RIGHTEOUSNESS PROTECTS MY SOUL;
SO I CAN STAND WHY EVIL COMES.

MY FEET ARE SHOD WITH THE GOSPEL OF PEACE.
THE LORD ABOVE I'LL SOMEDAY MEET.
MY FEET ARE SHOD WITH THE GOSPEL OF PEACE;
SO I CAN STAND WHEN EVIL COMES.

MY SHIELD OF FAITH IS IN ITS PLACE;
TO HELP ME WIN THIS CHRISTIAN RACE.
MY SHIELD OF FAITH IS IN ITS PLACE;
SO I CAN STAND WHEN EVIL COMES,

A CROWN OF SALVATION IS ON MY HEAD.
IT SHIELDS MY MIND FROM SIN AND DREAD.
A CROWN OF SALVATION IS ON MY HEAD;
SO I CAN STAND WHEN EVIL COMES.

THE SWORD OF THE SPIRIT IS IN MY HAND.
THE SWORD IS GOD'S WORD TO MORTAL MAN.
THE SWORD OF THE SPIRIT IS IN MY HAND;
SO I CAN STAND WHEN EVIL COMES.

I HAVE GOT ON THE WHOLE ARMOR OF GOD.
I HAVE GOT ON THE WHOLE ARMOR OF GOD.
I HAVE GOT ON THE WHOLE ARMOR OF GOD;
SO I CAN STAND WHEN EVIL COMES.

CLIFFORD BROWNER
C MAJOR
9/98
FROM THE COLLECTION "FIRST BLOOD"

TIL JESUS COMES

I'M GOING TO PRAY TIL JESUS COMES.

I'M GOING TO PRAY TIL JESUS COMES.

I'M GOING TO PRAY TIL JESUS COMES;

TIL I HEAR MY LORD, SAY WELL DONE.

I'M GOING TO LOVE WITH A CHRISTIAN'S LOVE.

I'M GOING TO LOVE WITH A CHRISTIAN'S LOVE.

I'M GOING TO LOVE WITH A CHRISTIAN'S LOVE;

TIL I HEAR MY LORD, SAY WELL DONE.

I'M GOING TO RUN TIL MY RACK IS WON.

I'M GOING TO RUN TIL MY RACE IS WON.

I'M GOING TO RUN TIL MY RACE IS WON;

TIL I HEAR MY LORD, SAY WELL DONE.

I'M GOING TO WORK TIL MY WORK IS DONE.

I'M GOING TO WORK TIL MY WORK IS DONE.

I'M GOING TO WORK TIL MY WORK IS DONE;

TIL I HEAR MY LORD, SAY WELL DONE.

I'M GOING TO STAY ON THE BATTLEFIELD.

I'M GOING TO STAY ON THE BATTLEFIELD.

I'M GOING TO STAY ON THE BATTLEFIELD;

TIL I HEAR MY LORD, SAY WELL DONE.

I'M GOING TO WAIT TIL JESUS COMES.

I'M GOING TO WAIT TIL JESUS COMES.

I'M GOING TO WAIT TIL JESUS COMES;

TIL I HEAR MY LORD, SAY WELL DONE.

CLIFFORD BROWNER

C MAJOR

1998

FROM THE COLLECTION "FIRST BLOOD"

TOUCH ME LORD
(AM BM EM AM)

COME ON DOWN AND TOUCH ME, LORD.

COME ON DOWN AND TOUCH ME, LORD.

COME ON DOWN AND TOUCH ME, LORD;

1T FEELS LIKE FIRE WHEN YOU TOUCH ME, LORD.

IT FEELS LIKE FIRE WHEN YOU TOUCH ME, LORD.

IT FEELS LIKE FIRE WHEN YOU TOUCH ME, LORD.

IT FEELS LIKE FIRE WHEN YOU TOUCH ME, LORD;

COME ON DOWN AND TOUCH ME LORD.

1) I CAN'T DO NOTHING

TIL YOU TOUCH ME, LORD.

2) I FEEL LIKE SHOUTING

WHEN YOU TOUCH ME, LORD.

3) I FEEL LIKE RUNNING

WHEN YOU TOUCH ME LORD.

4) I FEEL THE SPIRIT

WHEN YOU TOUCH ME, LORD.

REFRAIN:

(COME ON DOWN AND TOUCH ME LORD.)

IT FEELS LIKE FIRE, (IT FEELS LIKE FIRE)
IT FEELS LIKE FIRE, (IT FEELS LIKE FIRE)
IT FEELS LIKE FIRE, (IT FEELS LIKE FIRE)
IT FEELS LIKE FIRE, (IT FEELS LIKE FIRE)...

IT FEELS LIKE FIRE WHEN YOU TOUCH ME LORD.
IT FEELS LIKE FIRE WHEN YOU TOUCH ME LORD.
IT FEELS LIKE FIRE WHEN YOU TOUCH ME LORD.
COME ON DOWN AND TOUCH ME, LORD.

C. D. BROWNER 9/12/00
AM

TRY ME

TRY ME FATHER; (TRY ME)

TRY ME FATHER; (TRY ME LORD)

TRY ME FATHER; WON'T YOU (TRY ME)

CHORUS:

MY SOUL WON'T REST UNTIL YOU TRY ME LORD.

MY SOUL WON'T REST UNTIL YOU TRY ME LORD.

WHEN I'M DOWN, (TRY ME)

BURDENED DOWN, (TRY ME LORD)

WHEN I'M DOWN, LORD (TRY ME)

WHEN I'M SICK, (TRY ME)

CAN'T GET WELL, (TRY ME LORD)

WHEN I'M SICK, LORD (TRY ME)

WHEN I'M MOTHERLESS, (TRY ME)

WHEN I'M MOTHERLESS, (TRY ME LORD)

WHEN I'M MOTHERLESS, (TRY ME)

WHEN I'M FATHERLESS, (TRY ME)

WHEN I'M FATHERLESS, (TRY ME LORD)

WHEN I'M FATHERLESS, (TRY ME)

(INSTRUMENTAL)

YOU TRIED DAVID, (TRY ME)
AND PAUL AND SILAS (TRY ME LORD)
YOU TRIED JOB, WON'T YOU (TRY ME)

YOU TRIED DANIEL, (TRY ME)
THE HEBREW CHILDREN, (TRY ME LORD)
YOU TRIED MOSES, WON'T YOU (TRY ME)

YOU TRIED MY MOTHER, (TRY ME)
YOU TRIED MY FATHER, (TRY ME LORD)
TRY ME FATHER, (TRY ME)

TRY ME FATHER, (TRY ME)
TRY ME FATHER, (TRY ME LORD)
TRY ME FATHER, (TRY ME LORD)

MY SOUL IS READY, (TRY ME)
MY SOUL IS READY, (TRY ME LORD)
MY SOUL IS READY, (TRY ME)

I'LL DO YOUR WILL, (TRY ME)
I'LL DO YOUR WILL, (TRY ME LORD)
I'LL DO YOUR WILL, WON'T YOU (TRY ME)

UNTIL HE CALLS MY NAME

LORD ON THIS CHRISTIAN JOURNEY,

I FOUND SIN IN EVERY MAN.

I WANT TO BE LIKE JESUS;

I'VE GOT MY SWORD IN MY HAND.

LORD, I'M A CHRISTIAN SOLDIER,

AND I'M FIGHTING FOR MY CROWN.

I WANT TO HEAR THE CAPTIAN SOLDIER

TELL ME TO LAY MY ARMOR DOWN.

GOD IS FAITH, HOPE AND LOVE.

HE HEALS THE SICK AND THE LAME.

IF YOU REALLY WANT TO SEE JESUS

JUST TRUST IN HIS HOLY NAME.

I KNOW THAT GOD IS MY FORTRESS.

HE IS LORD TO EVERY MAN.

AND WHEN I'M FALLING DOWN,

THE LORD BUILDS ME UP AGAIN.

CHORUS:

I WANT TO WALK (LIKE JESUS).

I WANT TO TALK, (LIKE THE LORD).

I'M GONNA, (SERVE HIM, SERVE HIM,

SERVE HIM, UNTIL HE CALLS MY NAME).

(SING AFTER LAST CHORUS TO END SONG):

I WANT TO LOVE (EVERY BODY).

I WANT TO TREAT (MY NEIGHBOR RIGHT).

I WANT TO RUN (AND NEVER GET TIRED).

I WANT TO THINK HIM (FOR MY LIFE).

I'M GOING TO SERVE HIM, (SERVE HIM), SERVE HIM,

(UNTIL HE CALLS MY NAME).

C. D. BROWNER

FROM THE COLLECTION "QUIET PRAISE"

8/25/99

WASHED IN YOUR BLOOD

LORD I REMEMBER,

SO MANY YEARS AGO,

TO THE WATER I WAS TAKEN

IN A WHITE SHINY ROBE.

I WAS BAPTIZED IN THE WATER.

THE PREACHER PRAYED FOR MY SOUL

HE SAID THAT,

THERE CAN BE NO CLEANSING,

TIL I'M WASHED IN YOUR BLOOD,

WASHED IN YOUR BLOOD.

LORD I'M NOT WORTHY,

ALTHOUGH YOU DIED TO SAVE MY SOUL

HOW CAN I CLEANSE THIS BODY?

HOW CAN I CLEANSE MY SOULS?

I PRAY SOMEDAY I'LL FIND YOU

AND YOU'LL WASH AND MAKE ME WHOLE,

FOR THERE CAN BE NO CLEANSING

TIL I'M WASHED IN YOUR BLOOD,

WASHED IN YOUR BLOOD.

GOD IS REDEEMER.

HE SAVED ME WITH HIS LOVE.

HE MADE HIS HOME IN GLORY,

PLACED MY NAME UPON THE ROLL.

HE CHOSE A MAN CALLED NOAH,

WHO LIVED THROUGH THE FLOOD.
SO HIS CHOOSEN PEOPLE
COULD BE WASHED IN YOUR BLOOD,
WASHED IN YOUR BLOOD.

I AM TOLD
IT'S SO SIMPLE
THIS EVERY CHRISTIAN KNOWS.
MY FATHER UP IN HEAVEN
GAVE HIS HOLY WORD;
WHETHER BAPTIZED IN THE WATER
OR WASHED IN A FLOOD,

HE SAID THAT, THERE CAN BE NO CLEANSING
TIL I'M WASHED IN YOUR BLOOD,
WASHED IN YOUR BLOOD.

C. D. BROWNER, JR.
11/18/98
C MAJOR
FROM THE COLLECTION "FIRST BLOOD"

YOU ARE MY FRIEND

YOU ARE THE ONE
WHO'S ALWAYS THERE;
TO DRY AWAY MY TEARS.
YOU ARE THE ONE
I'VE LEANED ON;
THROUGH OUT THE TROUBLE YEARS.
YOU ARE THE ONE
I CALL ON;
WHEN NO ONE ELSE WILL HEAR.
I CRY LORD, OH LORD, OH LORD, OH LORD,
OH LORD, PLEASE HEAR MY PLEA?

YOU ARE THE ONE
WHO'S ALWAYS NEAR;
TO DRIVE AWAY MY FEARS.
AND NOW I KNOW
THE TIME HAS COME;
TO SAY YOU ARE MY FRIEND.
LORD, YOU ARE MY FRIEND;
UNTIL THE END.
I KNOW YOU ARE MY FRIEND.
YOU ARE MY FRIEND UNTIL THE END.
I KNOW YOU ARE MY FRIEND.

YOU STOOD BY ME
THROUGH THICK AND THIN.
I KNOW YOU ARE MY FRIEND.
YOU HELD MY HAND
THROUGH THE STORM AND RAIN.
I KNOW YOU ARE MY FRIEND.
YOU FORGIVE MY SIN;
TIME AND TIME AGAIN.
I KNOW YOU ARE MY FRIEND.
LORD, YOU ARE MY FRIEND
UNTIL THE END.

I KNOW YOU ARE MY FRIEND;
MY FRIEND, MY FRIEND, MY FRIEND.

CLIFFORD BROWNER
C MAJOR
3/96
FROM THE COLLECTION "FIRST BLOOD"

BLUE AND LOVE

SONG LYRICS

C. D. Browner, Jr.

DOWN IN GEORGIA

DOWN IN GEORGIA, I'VE GOT MEMORIES.
DOWN IN GEORGIA, I'VE GOT MEMORIES,

WHERE MIGHT IS RIGHT AND COTTON IS KING,
PEOPLE SO POOR, IT'S A DOG GONE SHAME,
OLD FOLKS CALLING ON JESUS' NAME,
DOWN IN GEORGIA.
I WENT TO SCHOOL IN A ONE-ROOM SHACK.
I MADE MY LIVING WITH AN OLD COTTON SACK,
THE RED HOT SUN SHINING ON MY BACK,
DOWN IN GEORGIA. I'VE GOT MEMORIES.
DOWN IN GEORGIA, I'VE GOT MEMORIES.

I LEFT HOME ON A TRAILWAYS BUS,
LEAVING FIELDS OF COTTON IN A CLOUD OF DUST,
LEAVING MY MOTHER'S LOVE AND MY FATHER'S TRUST,
DOWN IN GEORGIA.
WHAT KIND OF LIVING CAN YOU HOPE TO MAKE,
PICKING SHORT-NAP COTTON AT A TWO DOLLAR RATE,
SUN SO HOT YOUR SKIN WILL BAKE,
DOWN IN GEORGIA? I'VE GOT MEMORIES.
DOWN IN GEORGIA, I'VE GOT MEMORIES.

MY FAMILY SHARE-CROPPED A ONE-HORSE FARM,
WITH NO RUNNING WATER OR TELEPHONE.
I COULDN'T WAIT TIL I GOT GROWN,

DOWN IN GEORGIA.

MY HEART IS CARRYING A HEAVY LOAD.

I CAN'T GO TO HEAVEN TIL I FIND MY SOUL.

MY LIFE GOT STARTED ON AN OLD DIRT ROAD,

DOWN IN GEORGIA. I'VE GOT MEMORIES.

DOWN IN GEORGIA, I'VE GOT MEMORIES.

C. D. BROWNER, JR.

7/14/99

EM

FROM THE COLLECTION "BLUES FOR SUNDAY"

EVERLASTING LOVE

MY HEART'S ON FIRE, I LOSE CONTROL,
EACH TIME YOU REACH FOR THE DOOR,
CAUSE MAYBE YOU'RE LONGING TO BE FREE,
OR LOOKING FOR A CHANCE TO BE ALONE,
WHILE YOU'RE SEARCHING,
FOR YOUR EVERLASTING LOVE.
UH HUH, YOUR EVERLASTING LOVE.

I'M SURE MY LOVE, WE ALREADY KNOW
A LOVE MORE PRECIOUS THAN GOLD,
AND MAYBE OUR HEARTS ARE ALREADY FREE,
CAUSE WE HAVE EACH OTHER TO HOLD.
I PRAYED, FOR YOUR EVERLASTING LOVE;
I THANK GOD FOR YOUR EVERLASTING LOVE.
UH HUH, YOUR EVERLASTING LOVE.

ROMANTIC LOVE, A GIFT FROM ABOVE,
TWO HEARTS UNITED IN LOVE.
WE PLEDGE OUR HEARTS TIL DEATH DO US PART,
TWO HEARTS THAT WILL NEVER GROW COLD.
I PRAYED FOR YOUR EVERLASTING LOVE,
I THANK GOD FOR YOUR EVERLASTING LOVE.
UH HUH, YOUR EVERLASTING LOVE.

MY HEART'S ON FIRE, IT WARMS MY SOUL
TO BE THE ONE YOU LONG TO HOLD.
AND THIS ENDLESS LOVE, BLESSED UP ABOVE,
IT'S YOU I REALLY, REALLY LOVE.
I'VE FOUND MY EVERLASTING LOVE,
I THANK GOD FOR YOUR EVERLASTING LOVE,
UH HUH, YOUR EVERLASTING LOVE.

GENTLY

GENTLY, FRIENDSHIP GREW AND CHANGED TO LOVING,

WE FELL SO DEEP IN LOVE RIGHT FROM THE START.

I DREAMED OF YOU EACH NIGHT IN SWEET SURRENDER

AND LOVED YOU TO THE RHYTHM OF MY HEART.

QUIETLY, AS I WATCH YOU LAY THERE SLEEPING,

I CAN FEEL THE LOVE THAT LIVES IN YOUR HEART.

THE PEACE I KNOW WILL COME WITH EACH TOMORROW,

LET'S ME KNOW HOW TRULY BLESSED WE ARE.

TO KISS AND DANCE MAKES MEMORIES EVERLASTING;

THEY BIND TWO LOVER'S BODY, MIND, AND SOUL.

I'LL GIVE YOU ALL MY LOVE WITHOUT YOUR ASKING

LIKE THE SUN GIVES SUNSHINE TO A ROSE.

AND FROM NOW ON I'LL BUILD MY WORLD AROUND YOU,

AND IF BY CHANCE I EVER MADE YOU CRY,

I'LL HOLD YOU THROUGH THE NIGHT, MY PRECIOUS DARLING,

AND GENTLY KISS THE TEARDROPS FROM YOUR EYES.

HELPLESSLY, I WATCHED US TEAR TO PIECES,

A BEAUTIFUL AND PERFECT ROMANCE.

DESPERATELY, I'M SEARCHING FOR A REASON

WHY TWO HEARTS IN LOVE REFUSE TO DANCE.

I CALLED YOU YESTERDAY, TO SAY I'M SORRY.

I'VE CRIED EACH NIGHT SINCE WE'VE BEEN APART.

CAN'T YOU SEE I LOVE YOU STILL MY DARLING,

AND BEING WITHOUT YOU TRULY BREAKS MY HEART.

I LOVE YOU MORE THAN LIFE, MY PRECIOUS DARLING,
MY WORLD IS EMPTY, WHEN WE ARE APART. GRACEFULLY,
WE'LL DANCE AWAY THIS SORROW,
AND GENTLY, PUT THE LOVE BACK IN OUR HEARTS.

GOOD-BYE 1999

WITH JOY AND TEARS,
WE LEAVE THE PAST BEHIND.
YOUR TIME HAS COME,
BUT YOU'RE STILL ON MY MIND.
GOOD-BYE 1999, GOOD-BYE 1999

YOU'VE BEEN A YEAR
OF MANY UPS AND DOWNS.
WITH PAULA JONES AND MONICA,
WE HAD A GRANDE OLE TIME:
GOOD-BYE 1999, GOOD-BYE 1999

OUR CHILDREN LAUGHED;
OUR CHILDREN CRIED;
AND DIED AT COLUMBINE,
IN KOSOVO, THE DEAD WAS LEFT BEHIND.
GOOD-BYE 1999, GOOD-BYE 1999

WE ARE PRAYING FOR
A BETTER WORLD THIS TIME:
FILLED WITH LOVE
AND FREE OF VIOLENT CRIME.
GOOD-BYE 1999, GOOD-BYE 1999

C. D. Browner, Jr.

SOME PEOPLE FEAR
WE'RE NEAR THE END OF TIME.
THE NEW MILLENNIUM
IS HEAVY ON OUR MINDS.
GOOD-BYE 1999, GOOD-BYE 1999

CENTURY 21,
100 YEARS IN TIME,
NO MATTER WHAT WE'VE DONE,
THE BEST IS YET TO COME.
GOOD BYE 1999, GOOD-BYE 1999

WE ALL LOVE
THE THINGS YOU LEFT BEHIND:
MOVIE STARS, RODEOS,
AND FUNNY LOOKING CLOWNS;
GOOD-BYE 1999, GOOD-BYE 1999
GOOD-BYE 1999, GOOD-BYE 1999

CLIFFORD BROWNER
E MAJOR
6/1/95
FROM THE COLLECTION
"SONGS FROM THE HEART"
COPYRIGHTS RESERVED 1999

I FELL IN LOVE IN MINNESOTA

I FELL IN LOVE
IN MINNESOTA;
NEAR MANKATO
AT A WATERFALL.
MY LOVE AND I,
ONE SUMMER MORNING,
QUIETLY AWOKE,
TO A RAVEN CALL.

SUMMER NIGHTS ARE WARM
IN MINNESOTA
WITH A MUSIC SOUND,
ALL OF THEIR OWN.
TEN THOUSAND LAKES
ARE IN MINNESOTA,
WHERE THE SOUNDS OF BLACKNESS
MAKE THEIR HOME.

WE MADE NEW FRIENDS
IN MINNESOTA.
WE WALKED AND TALKED
ALL EVENING LONG.
MY FRIENDS AND I,
ONE SUNDAY MORNING,
WITNESSED ALTAR CALL
IN OLD ST. PAUL

I FELL IN LOVE
IN MINNESOTA.
I'M GOINC BACK
SOMETIMES NEXT FALL.
MY LOVE AND I,
AT MALL AMERICA,
WILL WINE AND DINE
AND HAVE A BALL.

I FELL IN LOVE
IN MINNESOTA,
MY WINNING SMILE,
SURE TELLS IT ALL.
I FELL IN LOVE
IN MINNESOTA,
WHERE A LOVE OF LIFE
GOES ON AND ON.

A MAJESTIC VIEW
OF THE OLD LANDMARKS,
ON THE COLDEST NIGHT,
STILL WARMS MY HEART.
SO GRAND AND LOVELY
IS MINNESOTA.
IN MINNESOTA
IS WHERE I FOUND MY HEART.

I'M YOUR MAN

NO ONE MISSES A GOOD THING;
UNTIL THAT GOOD THING IS GONE.
THEN THEY MISS HOW EASILY
YOU MADE A HOUSE A HOME.
THE ONE THAT YOU LOVED,
YOU SAY HE DID YOU WRONG.
IF YOU CARE TO TAKE A CHANCE,
BABY, I'M YOUR MAN.

YOU TOLD ME THAT YOU FELL IN LOVE,
TIME AND TIME AGAIN.
AND EVEN WHEN YOU FOUND TRUE LOVE,
YOU MADE NO WEDDING PLANS.
BUT IF YOU EVER NEED SOMEONE
WHO WILL LOVE AND UNDERSTAND,
IF YOU CARE TO TAKE A CHANCE,
BABY, I'M YOUR MAN.

YOU SAY YOU NEED SOMEONE TO WALK WITH YOU
IN THE SUMMER RAIN.
YOU SAY YOU NEED SOMEONE TO TALK TO YOU
WHEN YOUR HEART'S IN PAIN.
YOU SAY YOU NEED SOMEONE TO COMFORT YOU
AND HOLD YOUR TREMBLING HAND.
IF YOU CARE TO TAKE A CHANCE,
BABY, I'M YOUR MAN.

ON THOSE COLD AND LONELY NIGHTS
WHEN THE MOON IS YOUNG,
WHEN YOU NEED SOMEONE TO COMPORT YOU,
AND HOLD YOU IN HIS ARMS
AND GENTLY LOVE YOU THROUGH THE NIGHT
UNTIL THE MORNING COMES,
IF YOU CARE TO TAKE A CHANCE,
BABY, I'M YOUR MAN.

WHETHER IN THE SUMMER,
WINTER, SPRING OR FALL,
I PROMISE I WILL BE RIGHT THERE
TO ANSWER WHEN YOU CALL.
AND IF YOU EVER NEED SOMEONE
IN YOUR FUTURE PLANS,
IF YOU CARE TO TAKE A CHANCE,
BABY, I'M YOUR MAN.

SINCE WE MET, I'VE LONGED TO BE
THE LOVE OF YOUR LIFE.
SINCE WE MET, I THINK THAT I'VE
FOUND THE PERFECT WIFE.
WILL YOU COME AND GO WITH ME
TO BUY A WEDDING BAND?
IF YOU CARE TO TAKE A CHANCE,
BABY, I'M YOUR MAN BABY, I'M YOUR MAN.

MIDNIGHT LOVE

DAYLIGHT'S IN MY WINDOW, BABY;
I HEAR A MORNING DOVE.
I'M STILL FLYING HIGH
FROM YOUR AWESOME MIDNIGHT LOVE,

I HOPE YOU'RE READY, BABY;
I WANNA TAKE OUT MY FAVORITE GIRL.
YOU KNOW WE'VE GOTTA GET BACK EARLY
TO REST UP FOR SOME MIDNIGHT LOVE.

I SPENT ALL DAY ROLLING PENNIES, BABY,
TO BUY MYSELF A BOTTLE OF RUM.
YOU KNOW I GOTTA BE READY;
I GOTTA BE READY WHEN MIDNIGHT COMES.

DAYLIGHT'S IN MY WINDOW, BABY;
AND I THANK THE LORD ABOVE.
HE GAVE ME A SWEET WOMAN LIKE YOU
WITH A LOT OF MIDNIGHT LOVE.

IT'S NOONDAY IN THE VILLAGE, BABY,
LETS GO OUT AND HAVE SOME FUN.
YOU KNOW WE'RE GONNA BE LOVING
JUST AS SOON AS MIDNIGHT COMES.

IT'S TWELVE IN THE MORNING, BABY.

IT'S TIME FOR SOME MIDNIGHT LOVE.

WE'RE GONNA BE REELING AND ROCKING

UNTIL THE MORNING COMES.

CHORUS:

YOU CAN TEASE ALL YOU WANNA, BABY,

SIPPING ON THAT GLASS OF RUM,

AS LONG AS YOU BE READY,

READY WHEN MIDNIGHT COMES.

GIRL, YOU KNOW I'LL BE WAITING

FOR MY ROUND OF MIDNIGHT LOVE.

CLIFFORD BROWNER

7/13/99

FROM THE COLLECTION "BLUES FOR SUNDAY"

NOT YOU, NOT I, NOR ANYONE

THERE IS A BIBLE STORY
ABOUT GOD'S SERVANT JOB;
SATAN TOUCHED HIS BODY,
BUT GOD CONTROLLED HIS SOUL.
JOB WAS AFFLICTED FROM
HIS HEAD DOWN TO HIS TOES,
JOB PROCLAIMED HIS RIGTHEOUSNESS
AND QUESTIONED GOD'S CONTROL.

ELIHU A YOUNG MAN,
RESPECTED MEN OF OLD,
REBUKED JOB IN ANGER
AND WISDOM AS HE SPOKE.
HE SAID, I THOUGHT WITH
AGE YOU WOULD SPEAK; WITH
YEARS YOU WOULD TEACH
THE WISDOM THAT IS GOD'S,
THE BREATH OF GOD ALMIGHTY
GIVES COUNCIL TO THE YOUNG
AS WELL AS TO THE OLD.

ELIHU OPENED HIS MOUTH.
HIS HEART BEGAN TO SPEAK,
THE SPIRIT OF GOD HAS MADE ME,
HIS BREATH GAVE LIFE TO ME.
YOU SAY THAT GOD IS SILENT,

DEAF TO CRIES OF MAN.

JOB YOU ARE WRONG.

GOD IS GREATER THAN MAN.

GOD SPEAKS IN A VISION,

IN DREAMS TO SLEEP'N MAN.

HE WARNS THE SWORD IS JUSTICE

TO A SINFUL MAN.

OH ELIHU,

THE WORDS YOU SPOKE ARE TRUE,

NOT YOU, NOT I, NOR ANYONE

ARE GUILTLESS, CLEAN AND PURE.

OH ELIHU,

GOD IS BLESSING ME AND YOU.

NOT YOU, NOT I, NOR ANYONE,

ARE GUILTLESS, PURE AND TRUE.

C. D. BROWNER

10/25/99

OLD FRIEND

I SAW YOU YESTERDAY;
I WAS HAPPY.
I SAW YOU YESTERDAY;
I WAS GLAD.
IT'S BEEN TEN YEARS OR MORE
SINCE YOU MARRIED;
I LOST THE BEST FRIEND I EVER HAD.
OLD FRIEND, OLD FRIEND,
WHEN WILL THIS FEELING END?
YOU START A FIRE IN ME
THAT'S POTENT_
A FIRE SO HOT,
MY HEART'S ON OVERLOAD.
OLD FRIEND, OLD FRIEND,
WHEN WILL THIS FEELING END?
WHEN WILL WE LOVE AGAIN?

WE SHARED A LOVE
THAT HAD NO CONDITIONS;
A LOVE SO STRONG,
IT KNEW NO SUSPICIONS.
WELL, I KNOW NOW JUST WHAT
MY HEARTS BEEN MISSING;
I MISS LIKE HELL,
YOUR HOT JUICY KISSES.
THE FEELING WAS STRONG,

WHERE DID WE GO WRONG?

IT'S BEEN SO LONG,

I THOUGHT THE THRILL WAS GONE.

OLD FRIEND, OLD FRIEND,

WHEN WILL THIS FEELING END?

WHEN WILL WE LOVE AGAIN?

I MAY NEVER KISS

YOUR LIPS AS MY BRIDE

OR SHARE OUR SPECIAL LOVE

AS MAN AND WIFE,

BUT I NEED YOUR TOUCH;

I NEED YOUR SMILE;

I NEED YOU FOREVER IN MY LIFE.

OLD FRIEND, OLD FRIEND,

WHEN WILL THIS FEELING END?

WE'VE KISSED HELLO;

WE'VE KISSED GOOD-BYE;

I THOUGHT OUR KIND OF LOVE HAD DIED.

OLD FRIEND, OLD FRIEND,

WE'RE BACK IN LOVE AGAIN.

OLD FRIEND, OLD FRIEND,

WHEN WILL THIS FEELING END?

WHEN WILL WE LOVE AGAIN?

PIECES OF A DREAM

LIFE HAS BEEN SO WONDERFUl.

BETWEEN YOU AND ME;

I WONDER IF WE'RE LIVING

IN A WORLD OF MAKE BELIEVE.

KISS ME JUST DON'T WAKE ME

IF THIS IS A DREAM,

LET ME KEEP ON DREAM'N PIECES OF A DREAM.

I WORSHIP AND ADORE YOU,

MY SUNFLOWER QUEEN.

YOU RULE MY JOY, MY HAPPINESS

YOUR LOVE REIGN SUPREME.

YOU ARE MY MORNING COFFEE,

YOU'RE THE AIR THAT I BREATHE.

LET ME KEEP ON DREAM'N PIECES OF A DREAM.

I LIVE FOR THE MOMENT

WHEN YOU MAKE LOVE TO ME.

YOU TAKE AWAY MY LONELINESS

AND SET MY SPIRIT FREE.

PLEASE, DON'T EVER LEAVE ME,

OR WAKE ME FROM THIS DREAM.

LET ME KEEP ON DREAM'N PIECES OF A DREAM.

BEFORE YOU CAME INTO LIFE
EVERY DREAM I DREAM'D, WAS
FILLED SORROW AND REGRET,
AND SAD MEMORIES.
SINCE WE MET, MY DREAMS HAVE CHANGED;
LOVE IS IN MY LIFE.
I APPRECIATE THE LOVE YOU GIVE
AND EVERY SACRIFICE.
KISS ME JUST DON, T WAKE ME
FROM THIS PLEASANT DREAM;
LET ME KEEP ON DREAM'N PIECES OF A DREAM.

CHORUS:
PIECES OF A DREAM, PIECES OF A DREAM,
I CHERISH EVERY MOMENT, EVERY MEMORY.
KISS ME JUST DON'T WAKE ME, IF THIS IS A DREAM;
LET ME KEEP ON DREAM'N, PIECES OF A DREAM.
PIECES OF A DREAM, PIECES OF A DREAM,
LET ME KEEP ON DREAM'N PIECES OF A DREAM.

SOUTHERN LADY

SOUTHERN LADY,
WOMAN OF MY DREAM.
SHE'S A SOUTHERN LADY,
THIS WOMAN OF MY DREAM;
I'M GONNA GIVE HER TRUE LOVE
AND LOVE HER ENDLESSLY.

SHE'S A WARMHEARTED WOMAN,
THIS WOMAN OF MY DREAM.
SHE'S A WARMHEARTED WOMAN,
THIS WOMAN OF MY DREAM.
SHE'S A ONE MAN'S WOMAN,
AND SHE'S THE ONLY ONE FOR ME.

WHEN SHE WALKS DOWN THE STREET,
SHE'S A PURE DELIGHT TO SEE.
WHEN SHE WALKS DOWN THE STREET,
SHE'S A PURE DELIGHT TO SEE.
SHE'S A DIGNIFIED LADY,
AND LORD SHE BELONGS TO ME.

SHE'S GOT BEAUTY, BRAINS AND MORALS;
THE CUTEST THING I'VE EVER SEEN.
SHE'S GOT BEAUTY, BRAINS AND MORALS,
THE CUTEST THING I'VE EVER SEEN.
SO, COME ON SOUTHERN LADY;

PLEASE GIVE YOUR LOVE TO ME.

I'M GONNA BUILD YOU A HOME
ON A HILL BY THE SEA.
I'M GONNA BUILD YOU A HOME
ON A HILL BY THE SEA,
BUY YOU DIAMONDS, CARS, AND FURS
IF YOU SAY YOU'LL MARRY ME.

SOUTHERN LADY,
THIS WOMAN OF MY DREAMS.
SHE'S A SOUTHERN LADY,
THIS WOMAN OF MY DREAM.
SHE'S A ONE MAN'S WOMAN,
AND SHE'S THE ONLY ONE FOR ME.

SOUTHERN LADY,
THIS WOMAN OF MY DREAM.
SOUTHERN LADY,
THIS WOMAN OF MY DREAM.
YOU'VE GOT TO BE A SOUTHERN LADY
IF YOU WANT TO BE WITH ME.

CLIFFORD BROWNER
E MINOR

THE CLOSEST THING TO PERFECT

I GREW UP IN GEORGIA
ON THE WRONG SIDE OF TOWN.
I LEFT LOOK'N FOR A WOMAN
SO I COULD SETTLE DOWN.
I KNEW THE DAY I MET MARY
MY LIFE WOULD TURN AROUND; SHE'S THE CLOSEST THING
TO PERFECT I'VE FOUND.

I WENT LOOK'N FOR A WOMAN
WHO TRULY DID NOT MIND,
WASH'N, COOK'N, AND CLEAN'N
AND ONE WHO KNEW HOW TO IRON.
I LOOKED ALL OVER ATLANTA
AND THE SURROUND'N TOWNS;
I EVEN WENT OT ALABAMA,
BUT NOT ONE COULD BE FOUND.

SHE'S A HARD WORK'N WOMAN.
SHE'S RESPECTED AROUND TOWN.
SHE'S EDUCATED, SOPHISTICATED,
HER FEET ARE ON THE GROUND.
SHE'S A LOVING MOTHER.
SHE'S A SHININ' STAR.
SHE HAS HAD HER SHARE OF TROUBLE,
SHE HAS GOT SOME BATTLE SCARS.

I THOUGHT TO MYSELF
I WILL NEVER, NEVER FIND,
A WOMAN AS PERFECT,
AS THE ONE THAT IS IN MY MIND.
THEN ONE DAY I MET MARY
FROM THE OTHER SIDE OF TOWN,
SHE'S THE CLOSEST THING TO PERFECT
I'VE FOUND,

C. D. BROWNER, JR.
1/13/2000

TICK TOCK AROUND THE CLOCK

TICK TOCK AROUND THE CLOCK,
COME AND WATCH MY BODY ROCK
WE'LL PARTY HEARTY TIL WE DROP,
YOU JUST WATCH MY BODY ROCK.

WE DANCED ALL NIGHT THE NIGHT BEFORE,
PARTIERS KNOCKING AT MY DOOR.
THEY BEGGED AND PLEATED TO GE IN,
SO THEY COULD WATCH ME ROCK AGAIN.

THE MUSIC'S PUMPING LOUD AND SLOW,
LET THE PARTY PEOPLE ON THE FLOOR.
BODIES MOVING SMOOTH AND SLOW,
DJ! CRANK IT UP AND LET IT FLOW.

PARTY MUSIC FRESH AND CLEAR,
WE'RE DANCING WILDLY EAR TO EAR
WE CAN'T WAIT TIL THE PARTY ENDS,
SO WE CAN START IT UP AGAIN.

PARTY PEOPLE ON THE FLOOR,
CRANK IT UP A LITTLE BIT MORE.
KICK OFF YOUR SHOES AND JUMP RIGHT IN;
WE'RE BODY ROCKING TO THE END.

GANSTER ROCKERS ON THE FLOORS;
WE NEVER ROCKED THIS WAY BEFORE.
THE SECOND HAND IS MOVING FAST,
WHO KNOWS HOW LONG WE'RE GOING TO LAST.

WE'LL TOOTSIE ROLL AMONG THE STARS,
AND GANGSTER STROLL UP ON MARS.
WE CAN'T LET THIS PARTY STOP,
TIL MOM AND DAD DO THE BODY ROCK.

METHODICALLY, WE'RE TAKING TURN,
TIL SATURN RINGS BEGIN TO BURN.
BRO'S WOUND UP TIGHT THAT PARTY CLOCK,
AND LET THE LADIES BODY ROCK.

TICK TOCK AROUND THE CLOCK,
COME AND WATCH MY BODY ROCK.
WE'LL DANCE AND DANCE AROUND THE CLOCK,
YOU JUST WATCH MY BODY ROCK.

C. D. BROWNER, JR.
8/5/99

THE PLACE WHERE WE FELL IN LOVE

COME WITH ME
TO THE PLACE
WHERE OUR HEARTS
CAN BE FREE.
WHERE THE LOVE
WE SHARED LAST NIGHT
PLACED OUR HEARTS
ON A FLIGHT
TO THE PLACE
WHERE WE FELL IN LOVE.
TO THE PLACE,
WHERE WE FELL IN LOVE.

HOLD ME NEAR,
'TIL THE POUNDING
OF MY HEART DISAPPEARS.
QUIET THE WHISPERS
OF THE NIGHT,
OUR SIGHS OF LOVE,
WILL LEAD US BACK
TO THE PLACE,
WHERE WE FELL IN LOVE,
TO THE PLACE,
WHERE WE FELL IN LOVE.

HEAR MY PLEA;

DON'T LET NOTHING

COME BETWEEN YOU AND ME.

LET ME KISS

AND HOLD YOU TIGHT;

LOVE AND PASSION

WE'LL INVITE,

TO THE PLACE,

WHERE WE FELL IN LOVE.

TO THE PLACE,

WHERE WE FELL IN LOVE.

IF IT'S ME

THAT YOU NEED,

SAY YOU'LL SPEND

THIS NIGHT WITH ME.

I'LL BE YOURS

'TIL ETERNITY.

FOR IN LOVE,

WE JOIN TONIGHT.

OUR HEARTS WILL BE

THE GUIDING LIGHT,

TO THE PLACE,

WHERE WE FELL IN LOVE.

TO THE PLACE,

WHERE WE FELL IN LOVE.

C. D. BROWNER, JR.

YOU

YOU MADE LOVING YOU SO EASY;
I'M STILL GLOWING FROM THE THRILL.
YOU'RE THE VERY BREATH I'M BREATHING;
YOU ARE THE REASON THAT I LIVE.

THE TENDER LOVE THAT YOU'VE BEEN GIVING,
I NEED IT MORE EACH DAY I LIVE.
EACH KISS YOU GIVE IS A GIFT FROM HEAVEN.
YOU ARE THE REASON THAT I LIVE.

WITHOUT YOUR LOVE, I'D BE NOBODY,
I MIGHT AS WELL BE DEAD IN HELL.
THE SUN AND MOON WOULD BOTH STOP SHINING;
ONE DAY WOULD LAST A THOUSAND YEARS.

YOU'RE THE REASON I'M STILL DREAMING,
AND IF YOU FEEL THE LOVE I FEEL,
THERE'S NO WAY YOU'D BE LEAVING,
AND, YOU WOULD WEAR MY WEDDING RING.

YOU'RE THE CHANGING OF MY SEASONS,
YOU KNOW YOU MAKE MY WORLD STAND STILL.
OUR LOVE DEFY ALL SENSE OF REASONS;
YOU ARE THE REASON THAT I LIVE.

YOU ASK WHICH DAY IS WORTH RELIVING;
WELL, YESTERDAY WAS SAD AND BLUE,
TOMORROW JUST MIGHT BRING ME SORROW;
TODAY'S THE DAY I LOVE YOU.

I LOVE YOU, YOU, YOU, I LOVE YOU...

WALLS OF MY DREAMS

IT MAKES ME SO MAD I COULD SCREAM
WHEN I THINK AT LAST I'M ON A WINNING TEAM.
THEN SUDDENLY THE WOMAN THAT I LOVE
STARTS TEARING DOWN THE WALLS,
TEARING DOWN THE WALL OF MY DREAMS.

IT'S A MOMENTARY, TEMPORARY THING,
THE PAIN AND HEARTBREAK THAT THIS PROBLEM BRINGS.
WHEN SUDDENLY THE WOMAN THAT I LOVE,
STARTS TEARING DOWN THE WALLS,
TEARING DOWN THE WALLS OF MY DREAMS.

I'M A DREAMER,
I LIVE DEEP INSIDE OF MY DREAMS.
I'VE COME TOO FAR TO FALL APART,
TOO FAR TO MAKE A BRAND NEW START.
I'VE GOT TO FIND A WAY.
I'VE GOT TO FIND A WAY, TO STOP
THIS WOMAN THAT I LOVE,
THIS WOMAN THAT I LOVE,
FROM, TEARING DOWN THE WALLS,
TEARING DOWN THE WALLS OF MY DREAMS.

WHEN I THINK I'VE FOUND THE STRENGTH I NEED,

WHEN I THINK I'VE FOUND A WAY TO SUCCEED,

THEN SUDDENLY THE WOMAN THAT I LOVE

STARTS TEARING DOWN THE WALLS,

TEARING DOWN THE WALLS OF MY DREAMS.

IT'S A MOMENTARY, TEMPORARY THING,

THE PAIN AND HEARTBREAK THAT THIS PROBLEM BRINGS.

WHEN SUDDENLY THE WOMAN THAT I LOVE,

STARTS TEARING DOWN THE WALLS,

TEARING DOWN THE WALLS OF MY DREAMS.

CLIFFORD BROWNER

6/5/99

EM FORM

FROM THE COLLECTION "SONGS FROM THE HEART"

WE'VE BEEN FRIENDS

THRU THE YEARS,
DOWN THRU THE YEARS,
DOWN THRU THE YEARS
WE'VE BEEN FRIENDS.
THRU THE YEARS,
THRU THICK AND THIN,
FROM START TO END,
WE'VE BEEN FRIENDS.

YESTERDAY WAS FUN;
WE PLAYED HARD AND LONG.
SO LET TOMORROW COME,
WHAT'S DONE IS DONE.
BUT FOR TODAY
WE'LL SING THIS SONG,
DOWN THRU THE YEARS
WE'VE BEEN FRIENDS.

MEMORIES,
LIKE THE LIGHT OF DAY,
WHEN EVENING COMES
SOON FADE AWAY.
WE SHARED JOY AND PAIN
WEATHERED STORMS AND RAIN,
DOWN THRU THE YEARS
WE'VE BEEN FRIENDS,

(REPEAT FIRST STANZA)

FRIENDSHIP GROWS STRONG,
STRONGER DAY BY DAY,
WHEN TROUBLE COMES
NO ONE RUNS AWAY.
WE SHARED JOY AND PAIN,
WEATHERED STORMS AND RAIN,
DOWN THUR THE YEARS
WE'VE BEEN FRIENDS.

LOVE, FAITH AND TRUST
BETWEEN TRUE FRIENDS,
IS WORTH THE POT OF GOLD
AT THE RAINBOW END.
FRIENDSHIPS TRANSCEND
THE JOURNEY ENDS;
BUT UNTIL THEN
WE'VE BEEN FRIENDS.

C D. BROWNER 11/29/2000
G MAJOR
DEDICATED TO MY FRIEND, DENNIS WILLIAMS

ONE LINERS
AND QUOTES
FROM FRIENDS

C. D. Browner, Jr.

"QUOTES, ONE-LINERS AN FAVORITE SAYINGS OF EVERYDAY PEOPLE"

"BE YOURSELF, BEFORE YOU BE BY YOURSELF."

"IT CAN'T TALK, IT AIN'T SUPPOSE TO WIN."
THE LATE FRANK JOHNSON

"YOU'RE TRYING TO BRING THE WEAKEST S – TO THE STRONGEST PEOPLE." THE LATE FRANK JOHNSON

"IF YOU AIN'T GOT AN OLD MAN, YOU AIN'T GOT YOURSELF NOTHING." JOSEPH JOHNSON

"AIN'T GONNA BE NONE LEFT," JOSEPH JOHNSON REPLY CONCERNING HIS RAW BARBEQUED CHICKEN

"DRINK UP BOYS, I BOUGHT THIS WHISKEY TO DRINK." NOTE: WHEN JOSEPH JOHNSON RETURNED FORM THE MEN'S ROOM THE BOTTLE WAS EMPTY. THEY DIDN'T LEAVE HIM A DROP.

"I GOT MONEY'S MA, I GOT A HUNDRED AND A HUNDRED MORE" THE LATE "DO RIGHT" MICHEAL PICKETT

THE LATE "DO RIGHT" ABOUT HIS EX-WIFE; WHEN THE KIDS WERE YOUNG RECEIVING CHILDSUPPORT, SHE'D SAY, "THESE MY CHILDREN". WHEN THEY GREW UP AND STARTED KICKING HER

BEHIND; SHE SAID, "COME GIT YOUR CHILDREN". THE LATE "DO RIGHT" MICHEAL PICKETT

"AIN'T BUT A FEW GOOD MEN LEFT; ME, MY DADDY, AND MY BROTHER" SYLVESTER BROWNER

"...BETTER GET YOURS, I GOT MINE." JOSEPH JOHNSON

"YOU BETTER DO WHAT YOU CAN WHILE IT'S LIGHT; NO MAN CAN SEE AFTER DARK." SYLVESTER BROWNER

"A MONKEY WILL EAT PEPPER IF HE GETS HUNGRY ENOUGH" THE LATE, CLIFFORD BROWNER, SR.

"A MAN THAT WON'T WORK, WILL STEAL"

... ON WORKING ON SUNDAY. "I GOTTA GET MY OX OUT THE DITCH". SYLVESTER BROWNER

"A COW NEEDS ITS TAIL MORE THAN ONE FLY SEASON."
MRS. JOHNNIE L BROWNER

"IT'S SUCH AS IT IS."
THE LATE, "MOTHER IRA" MRS. IRA LOWE

"WHO WOULDN'T SERVE A GOD LIKE THIS?"
THE LATE ROBERT MULLIN, JR.

"MARK IT LIGHT ON YOUR SELF"
C. D. BROWNER, JR.

"A MANS GOTTA DO WHAT A MANS GOTTA DO"
C. D. BROWNER, JR

"SOME FOLKS'LL RIDE A FREE HORSE TO DEATH"
UNKNOWN

"PICK YOUR POISON"
UNKNOWN

"DON'T GIVE NOBODY MORE THAN YOU CAN WALK OFF AND
LEAVE" SYLVESTER BROWNER

"LOOKED LIKE ME; WASN'T ME. LOOKED LIKE LYNNE'S CAR;
WASN'T LYNNE'S CAR. I WASN'T THERE."
ERIC JONES

"WHATEVER MAKES YOU HAPPY"
C. D. BROWNER, JR

"REMEMBER, WHILE YOU ARE AT THE ZOO LOOKING AT THE
MONKEYS; THE MONKEYS ARE LOOKING AT YOU."
RAYMOND GERMON

"THE LAST PERSON I WANT TO FOOL IS MYSELF."
C. D. BROWNER, JR.

C. D. Browner, Jr.

"YOU BETTER SAVE YOURSELF. IF YOU DON'T NOBODY ELSE WILL"
SYLVESTER BROWNER

www.ingramcontent.com/pod-product-compliance
Lightning Source LLC
Chambersburg PA
CBHW051432280526
45785CB00003B/1263